Union and disunion, o. ne true
relation of the Church of
England to other religious
communities, Catholic and
Protestant : an address delivered
by request of the Salisbury
Branch of the English Church
Union, at Laverstock, on the
19th of August, 1869

John Henry Blunt 1823-1884

UNION AND DISUNION:

OR

THE TRUE RELATION

OF THE

Church of England

TO

OTHER RELIGIOUS COMMUNITIES,

CATHOLIC AND PROTESTANT.

An Address delivered by request of the Salisbury Branch of the English Church Union,

AT LAVERSTOCK, ON THE 19TH OF AUGUST, 1869.

BY THE

REV. JOHN HENRY BLUNT, M.A., F.S.A.,

VICAR OF KENNINGTON, OXFORD,
AUTHOR OF THE 'HISTORY OF THE REFORMATION,'
&c. &c. &c.

SALISBURY: BROWN & CO.
LONDON: SIMPKIN, MARSHALL, & CO.
1870.

SALISBURY :

BENNETT, PRINTER, JOURNAL OFFICE.

TO SIR EDWARD HULSE, BARONET,

Of Breamore House,

President of the South Wilts District Union of the English Church Union.

DEAR SIR EDWARD HULSE,

When the following words were spoken I did not suppose they would reach beyond the circle of those who listened to them. A request having, however, been sent to me by a subsequent Meeting of the Members that my address to them should be produced in a permanent form and for a wider circle, I have written it out for publication. In doing so, I venture to inscribe it to you, partly because you presided on the occasion of its delivery, and partly because you represent a class of laymen whose prudent judgement, and steady ecclesiastical loyalty, provide one great guarantee, under Divine Providence, that any movement towards Union between the Church of England and other religious communities, must be well considered, if it is to be successful, and not the result only of an impulsive zeal.

With much respect and regard, I beg to remain,

Dear Sir Edward Hulse,

Yours very truly,

J. H. BLUNT.

UNION AND DISUNION,

&c.

THERE are few greater difficulties to an ardent-minded Churchman of the present day than those presented by the want of unity in Christendom, and the apparent impossibility of any general return to what seems a first principle of Christianity. Within the narrow circle of a country town, or even of a village, there are to be found several Christian communities whose differences, however much they may be minimized by good-natured interpretations, are, in reality, so deeply seated as to be practically irreconcileable. Taking a wider circle, the Roman Communion is found utterly unwilling to hold out the right hand of fellowship to the Oriental or the Anglican, and yet to claim for itself a true and perfect Unity within its own borders. Is it consistent with the true principles of Christianity, with the article of the Creed which speaks of One Holy Catholic and Apostolic Church, or, above all, with the statements of the New Testament, and the prayers of our Lord, that there should be these divisions?

At the present time such thoughts are suggested to many in a form which is calculated to raise a comparison between the Anglican and the Roman Communions, in which the latter may appear in a much more favourable light as regards unity than the former. The grand spectacle of nearly a thousand bishops all wending their way to Rome and the Pope, as to a centre of unity acknowledged by them all in whatever part of the world they may be placed, is one that may well excite some degree of envy; and there is an obvious opportunity for contrasting such a spectacle with the isolated position of the Church and Episcopate of England. There are a great many of us who look regretfully upon the absence of our English bishops from the Vatican Council, and not a few who have a half feeling that the Church of England must be somehow in the wrong that it should thus be shut out. Such a feeling is also liable to be strengthened by the calm dogmatism with which the Pope and his councillors exclude us altogether from their enumeration of Christian Churches, assuming as a long foregone conclusion, that we have no part whatever in the One Body of Christ. Such assumptions do not indeed shake our belief in the Catholicity of the Church of England, but they do help to thicken that mist which prevents us from seeing at once the solid ground of true Union that underlies a large proportion of the divisions of Christendom.

It seems, therefore, to be a special time for recalling to mind what are the first principles on which Church Unity is established; that we may thus settle and solidify our ideas on the subject, forming some general opinion as to the extent to which we of the Church of England really are united to or disunited from the rest of Christendom.

In what, then, are we to look for the true and real signs of Unity between the various parts of the Church as a corporate section of a corporate whole? And in what are we to seek the true means of realizing that Unity? Are we to seek these in the external charities of ecclesiastical life by which Church holds intercourse with Church through the visible intercommunion of their individual members, the mutual exchange of their official documents, or the common consultation of their Bishops? And if these signs of Unity are absent, must we say that Unity is absent also?

Certainly these acts of intercourse are no unimportant features in the Unity of the Church: but they are not its efficient causes. It would be a great blessing for Christendom if such acts of Christian friendship could be revived, but they are not essential. They are, in fact, the growth of the Vine's leafage, not the growth of its fruit: and the thinning out of the leaves neither destroys the vital unity of the branches one with another nor diminishes the amount of spiritual produce that each branch may yield when the time of the vintage comes.

No: we must look deeper for the true Unity of the Church than to such acts of external Communion. The true bond of vital Union is the Life which is maintained by the Presence of Christ: and that Pre-

sence is obtained for each Church not by acts of
fellowship towards other Churches but by acts which
maintain the fellowship of each with the Fountain of
Sacramental grace.   Acts of external fellowship are
the result of many wills all tending to one point; but
Sacraments represent the one will of the Church—not
of individual priests or of individual recipients—co-
operating with the Will of GOD.   Thus it is the work
of the Holy Ghost in effecting the Presence of Christ
which produces the real Unity of the Church, as it
produces its real life.   But the Holy Ghost effects
this work, we know, by means of the external agency
of a valid Priesthood and of the valid Form and
Matter of the Holy Eucharist.   When these are in
action, whether in the Church of England, or the
Church of France, or the Church of Rome, or the
Church of Constantinople, or the Church of Jeru-
salem, or the Church of Abyssinia, or the several
Churches of North and South America, there Christ
becomes present, and no human power or will can
prevent Him from being present.   What a perfect
bond of Unity, then, is thus originated !   If He thus
becomes present in the Church of England, thus in
the Church of France, thus in the Churches of Italy,
Greece, Russia, Palestine, Africa, and America, what
more effectual Unity of those Churches can there be
than that Objective Unity which is thus accomplished
by the Presence in each of His One Indivisible Person ?   Breaches of charity may make that Presence

inefficacious for the particular sanctification of those who are guilty of them, but I do not see what there can be that can make corporate Union between Churches more *real*, though I see many things that might make it more *evident.*

I will endeavour to strengthen this line of argument by an illustration drawn from the opposite point of view. Suppose the case, that the Holy Eucharist was, as some believe, only a sign of fellowship between man and man, and that our Lord was associated with it only as He is associated with acts of prayer. It is quite plain that there could then be no union between Churches by means of it, except through the communion of the individual communicants of whom the respective Churches were made up. In that case, if the individual communicants of the Church of A all broke off communion with the individual members of the Church of B, then indeed there would be an entire dissolution of the bond of unity. If that were the case, for example, with the Eucharists of the Churches of Rome and England, then an entire failure of acts of communion would be equivalent to an entire separation of the two Churches.

But such a principle as that supposed reverses the whole order of unity. The members of Christ, the branches of the Vine, the living stones of the Temple, are in union with each other by virtue of Christ's Presence in them. It is not the *Subjective expression of oneness* that unites them but the *Objective actual oneness of the Body of Christ.* The subjective expressions of oneness,—such as appearance of unity, loving words, common organization, mutual ecclesiastical intercourse,—these may be altogether wanting as they must be in a multitude of cases where Christians are not ever brought within the same circle of kindred, acquaintance, or nationality, and yet the Objective Presence of the Indivisible Person may be effecting a most real, true, and perfect union between them. On the other hand, if that Objective Presence is not in them, no subjective expressions of union will ever bring, or ever truly indicate, the real unity of a common Christian vitality.

As it is with individual Christians so it is with Churches. That which can drive Christ out of Churches can separate them from Him: and that which can separate a particular Church from Him separates it from other Churches. But so long as He is present in each they must be in union with each other, let what may be said to the contrary.

Thus, then, whatever our respective sins and misunderstandings may do—and I have no wish to understate their miserable results—in breaking off external communion between particular parts of the One Mystical Body, there is still the hope, and a strong hope, that these sins have not, on either side, gone so far as to drive out the Living Presence. And a strengthening of the conviction that this Living Presence is in two apparently dissevered branches of the Church may tend to soften down the effects of outward divisions, perhaps to promote their extinction. The want of faith in that Presence among English people has probably been one great cause of our ecclesiastical isolation; and a corresponding want of faith in our possession of It, on the part of un-historical and illogical Romanists, has co-operated towards the same end. And if this is so, then it follows that the restoration of Unity is to be sought, not by intertwining branches, but by giving to each branch a more complete and universal current of that Life which comes from the life-giving Root and Stem: not by endeavouring to make or re-establish arrangements by which the walls of the fabric may be brought into apparent conformity and artistic symmetry, but by removing all that weakens their stability, and by promoting all that brings about the fulness and freedom of the exercise of Christ's vitalizing power.

Having thus recalled to our recollection what is the true principle of Christian Unity, I will venture to draw attention to some historical considerations which seem to me to tend very much towards making us less discontented with the apparent divisions of Christendom.

Such divisions, it seems to me, are the result in a very great degree, of political circumstances rather than of religious dissensions; or of religious dissensions not in themselves of very high importance but aggravated by political hostility.

The Church was most *visibly* one when the world owned allegiance to one civil head. Even in the days of greatest purity it was no feeble auxiliary that the Apostles had to their work when they could pass from one nation to another and found national Churches among peoples who had one Imperial unity. And when the age of persecution arrived the heavy hand of the civil power compressed all separate interests of individual Churches into one by the danger of it which was common to all, and which often, doubtless, as in the case of the early stage of the Paschal controversy, stayed the progress of enmities that might soon have developed in times of tranquil safety.

Then came the age of Councils, an age of terrible divisions which eventually culminated in Mahometanism and the desolation of the Eastern Church. And yet, in the midst of wide spread heresies like those of Sabellianism and Arianism—with all their subtle developments and ramifications—those Councils which offered the most striking picture of Church Unity that was ever exhibited were assembled with the greatest facility. Why could they be thus assembled then, and never since then? Why but because there was an Imperial power that had authority to call together any class of its subjects, that could provide for their meeting in one common assembly as subjects of one common temporal Sovereign, and that could exercise a control over them by means of their one common allegiance. This may seem a very low view to take of our great Councils, but can we see our way to the assembly of a really general Council from any other point of view? Is there any Council since the days of the United Empire that an impartial historian will be willing to call 'general' in the same high degree as those which were held before its disintegration? I venture, then, to repeat, that the Unity of the Empire of Rome was an important element in the early visible Unity of the Church, and to add that the loss of the one entailed to a large extent the loss of the other.

It is true that the centralising power of the Empire was in some degree inherited by the Court of Rome, the traditions of the Imperial City of which the Pope was Bishop giving him an Imperial *prestige* which he would never have possessed through his ecclesiastical position alone. But the further we come down the stream of history, the more discord we find arising out of that Papal inheritance. The world receded from the idea of an Universal Empire, and the claims of Imperial authority on the part of the Bishops of Rome were necessarily in conflict with the claims of national independence. Hence Rome failed to keep together the Eastern and Western Churches. Hence, later on the struggles always kept up on the part of France and England against the assumed jurisdic-

tion of the Popes, even when there was no discord as
to the doctrine and internal discipline of the several
Churches. Hence, still later, that strong current of
division which set in with the sixteenth century,
floating on its surface the scum of many an error, and
overwhelming many a goodly institution in its rushing
whirl. Is it a mere unhistorical imagination that
Roman Ecclesiasticism alone would never have set
this current of division astir, and that the mischief
was done by Roman Imperialism ? or is it not rather
a conclusion forced upon us by a just and broad ob-
servation of the course of events, distinguishing (as
English statesmen of the Mediæval and Reformation
periods always distinguished) between the action of
the Ecclesiastical *Court* of Rome and the action of
the Spiritual *Church* of Rome ?

From the very beginning of its existence, then, the
Catholic Church has been largely influenced as to the
external relations to each other of its several national
branches by the political circumstances of the countries
in which those branches are nationalized. And one
consequence has been that the Churches of Christendom have broken asunder from each other not so
much on account of irreconcileable spiritual differences
as through the necessities of national life which run
side by side with ecclesiastical life. Could the political unity of the world be restored, and national
independence brought as low as it was in the days of
the Empire, some of the greatest obstacles to visible

ecclesiastical unity would be abolished. But separate nationalities have been established by GOD's good Providence. The only universal Empire we now look for is that of Antichrist, and when that comes the diminishing remnant of the Church will doubtless be purified and outwardly united as in the time of primitive distress and suffering.

And now the question arises, What is our practical duty in respect to the promotion of Unity? What does Christian expediency suggest as to the diminution of our divisions? It may be that those divisions are not of so vital a character as we have sometimes supposed : it may be that the world has been so ordered by GOD's providential disposition of events that the external Unity of early days can never be restored. But can nothing be done? Can we not establish a more visible union with the Eastern Churches? Is the new-born political friendship of Englishmen and Frenchmen to have no parallel in their ecclesiastical relations? Does Rome itself hopelessly withhold the right hand of fellowship? And then, again, in the case of our domestic divisions, can no union be effected between the Church and the Dissenters?

I confess to thinking that the present generation will be able to do nothing whatever of a *direct* nature towards the promotion of visible union between our own and other Churches as corporate bodies, although all that is being done towards Church revival is in reality a preparation for closer fellowship, and our children may live to build on our foundations.

But a most necessary work towards that end, it seems to me, next to that of reviving Church life within our own borders, is that of re-establishing on a sound footing the theological position of the Church of England. In past times England has sold herself into the hands of a religious literature which was very far from representing the true doctrine of the Church of England; and the consequence is we have been altogether misunderstood by the Catholic world. The Conservative East has looked on the Church of England as a community of Sadducæan free-thinkers. The formal ecclesiasticism of the West has identified us with Lutheranism, Calvinism, and the misbegotten ideal of a 'Parliamentary Church' which has been set forth as our true portrait by many English writers. How can it be expected that the East or the West should be willing to unite in visible communion with those of whom they learn to form such opinions? The very few points of agreement which we have with sects that are thorns in our sides have been thrust prominently forward: our far more numerous points of contact with the Roman Catholic world and the Eastern Churches have been carefully ignored; and what other result could be expected? It is indeed, a comfort to see a bold declaration of those points of contact such as is contained in the third part of Dr. Pusey's Eirenicon; but we want to be able to point to something more than a pamphlet : we want to be able to lay our hand upon a few scholarly volumes of Theology that will bear comparison with the great works of Benedictines and Jesuits, and to say Here is something more than mere popular religionism, here are true expositions of Anglican principles that we are not ashamed of, and that are worth your attention.

If we ever have such a body of Theological works as this, our doctrinal relations to the rest of the Catholic Church will appear in a very different light from that in which they have been exhibited hitherto, especially if statements of doctrine are kept clear from passion and polemics. It will then be seen that there is very little—as far as bulk goes, at any rate— of *old* Roman theology which is not substantially identical with Anglican theology ; though the Church of England does, indeed, emphatically decline to accept such novelties as extravagant theories about Transubstantiation. Purgatory, and the *cultus* of the Blessed Virgin.

But if Rome could ever be brought back from comparatively modern notions on such subjects as these to her formal standards of doctrine, the greatest obstacle to a good understanding between us would be set aside. If Roman theologians and Anglican theologians would consent to be honestly historical, and to accept Patristic and Early Scholastic Theology as the most Catholic exposition of Christian truth there would be little difficulty about a common faith.

It would be found that the difference between the Roman doctrine of Transubstantiation (stripped of its theory of annihilation) was not irreconcileable with the Anglican doctrine of the Real Presence,—of a new spiritual Substance engrafted upon the old natural substance ; that the Anglican middle state of waiting and purification and spiritual progress is not irreconcileable with the doctrine of Purgatory, when the latter is stripped of its mediæval accretions ; and that the Anglican veneration of her who became the Mother of GOD is only irreconcileable with Roman ideas respecting her when the latter pervert her true position into that of Deity. We may depend upon it that modern Roman theologians would learn a great deal from a sound exposition of Anglican theology, and would draw much nearer to us on account of it.

But a much more real difficulty than that of Roman Theology is that of Roman Schism. The weak submission of a few Englishmen to the influence of foreign ecclesiastics has caused the presence of a modern rival face to face with the ancient Church of England —a Roman invasion of the Church in possession which can be supported on Donatist principles, but not on Catholic principles. Thus we have the task of opposing the Schism of Romanism rather than its Theology: and unless this is done vigorously we either give up the title of the Church of England to her position, or let it lapse into a claim for mere joint possession.

As regards the schism of English Roman Catholics I do earnestly think it would promote the cause of true Unity if we were to take a much bolder line than it has been the custom to take. Almost the only 'High Churchman' who ever used properly strong language on this subject was Archdeacon Manning, who, in his admirable volume on the 'Unity of the Church,' (dedicated to Mr. Gladstone, in the year 1845,) tells the truth without flinching. 'The attempt' he writes 'to impose an uncanonical jurisdiction on the British Churches, and a refusal to hold communion with them except on that condition was clearly an act of schism. And this was further aggravated by every kind of aggression: acts of excommunication, and anathema, instigations to warfare abroad, and to rebellion and schism at home, are the measures by which the Roman Church has exhibited its professed desire to restore unity to the Church of Christ. It must never be forgotten that the act of the Bishop of Rome, by which a most grievous and stubborn contest was begun in the English Church was taken not in the character of patriarch, but of Supreme Pontiff. The same bull which made a rent in every English Diocese professed to depose also the Queen of England. It was a power to give away not sees, but thrones also; and the effect of this has been, as in the East so in England, to erect altar against altar, and succession against succession. In the formation of sects in diocesan Churches, in the exclusive assumption of the name Catholic, in the re-ordination of priests, and in restricting the One Church to their own communion, there has been no such example of division since the schism of Donatus.'* I will not water down these eloquent and true words by any expansion of their condensed truth. It is enough to add my conviction that nothing should prevent us from 'speaking out' in this bold tone as to the claims of the Church of England whenever occasion arises, and my confidence that we should, by doing so, gain respect, and convince many an opponent that those claims are just. We ought to make it plain that if there is ever to be union between England and Rome the first great step in the process must be the re-absorption of the Anglo-Roman sect into the English Church.

In dealing with the question of union between the Church of England and the Protestant sects of our country, there is no necessity, for the purpose before us, to go into the history of the past. It is enough to observe that the Dissenting sects—with one exception, the Irvingites—reject and are opposed to the Sacerdotal principle and the Sacramental system. But these are the very life of the Church of England system. The ministration of priests is as fundamental a principle in the Church of England, and is as carefully provided for, as it is in the Church of Rome;

* "The Unity of the Church. By Henry Edward Manning, M.A., Archdeacon of Chichester. Second Edition." London: Murray, 1845, p. 364.

and so is a Sacramental system which recognizes the conveyance of GOD's grace by means of external instruments as one of the most vital principles of Christianity. Shallow writers and platform talkers conjure up in their imagination some fanciful ideal of a Prayer Book without Sacerdotalism and without Sacramentalism; and even men who have done the best they could to get themselves ordained Priests have been heard to declare that they were not Priests at all, or only so in a 'non-natural sense.' And yet every one knows very well how strict the law is in forbidding any but Priests to celebrate the Holy Communion, and in preventing any but Priests from holding benefices: and if this is not Sacerdotalism, what is?

Here then are some broad lines on which the Church of England stands on the one hand, and sects of Dissenters on the other. Priesthood and Sacraments in no non-natural, but in their commonly-received sense, are essential features of the Church of England system; and, in that commonly-received sense, they are rejected by the systems of Protestant Dissenters. It is impossible, then, for the two to unite unless one or the other gives up their system. And, as it is mere surplusage to talk of the Church of England giving up her Priesthood and her Sacraments, the only possible pathway to Union with Methodists, Independents, or Presbyterians (to name no other sects) is on Sacerdotal principles. Let us say this to them firmly, instead of beating the air with talk about mutual concessions. How can we concede the necessity of Episcopal Ordination for the ministry, or of Sacerdotal acts of Consecration for the Eucharist? And if Protestant Dissenters do not consider these an obstacle to their union with the Church, what is it they do consider so? But the wiser men among them know very well that, however much some on either side may try to disguise the fact by flourishes about a 'common Protestantism,' the Sacerdotalism of the Church of England is a wall around it which Dissenters can neither beat down nor climb over, and that if they want to be within the city they must come in by the gate. They know also that it is as impossible for us to destroy this obstacle as for them to do so : that we have neither the right nor the power to give up the fundamental principles of the Church ; and that if union cannot now be effected in any other way than by doing so, we have only to bow our heads and wait patiently for better times, when some other way may be discovered.

Perhaps some may be disposed to say—What a hard view this is ! What a dreary and hopeless prospect this sort of reasoning opens out! What a wet blanket to throw over our ardent aspirations after Christian union? All I can say by way of apology is that truth often does present itself in the form of a rough and angular wall; and that attempts to make it more pleasant to the enemy by rubbing off its angles and polishing its surface will have little effect unless they also weaken its substance. We may talk smooth things about union to the Anglo-Romanist on the one hand or to the Protestant Dissenter on the other, but the truth must come out at last.

Yet, after all, I am not so sure that the prospect is so dreary and the truth so discouraging. Perhaps we are nearer to external and visible unity than we have been for some centuries, and perhaps our approach towards it is being facilitated by the growth of that out-spokenness, and that recurrence to first principles which I have been advocating. But above all, I believe that we are growing nearer to Union—in spite of all appearances to the contrary—by the imperceptible development of the Spiritual bond of the Divine Presence.

The fact is, that every religious movement of our day bears the stamp of the age, a want of patience. We live in too great a hurry, and look too soon for results. We try to gain by art, skill, and energy what is only to be gained by time, patience, and perseverance in waiting. The old wine which the chymistry of time produces is not to be imitated by all the brilliant processes of the laboratory : neither will the *forcing* of opinion and feeling produce the true and really valuable results which are brought about by the subtle moral chymistry that imperceptibly mellows the convictions of society.

I venture to say, therefore, in respect to this question of visible unity among Christians,—First, let us be patient; Secondly, let us be frank and bold as to the principles and claims of the Church of England; Thirdly, let us be loyal to the Church, not coquetting with either Romanists or Protestant Dissenters.

There seems, indeed, to be a Providential position assigned to the Church of England which may well encourage us as to her future work in the promotion of unity. A faithful development of her principles and practice exhibits her as a sufficient home for the most intellectual, the most devout, the sincerest lovers of spiritual discipline, the most ardent disciples of spiritual liberty; a sufficient home for the rich, and a sufficient home for the poor, for young and old, for wise and simple. Unyielding in the maintenance of fundamental truths, there is yet room within her walls for men who love free thought, and no 'Churchism' is so 'Broad' as that of the Church. Such being the case, there seems good reason to hope that the great Church of this great and wide-spread nation contains elements which are gradually developing her action as a mediating power among the divided portions of Christendom; and that her Theology and Ritual may prove to be the type of twentieth century Christianity as Roman Theology and Ritual were a pattern for that of the Middle Ages.

CPSIA information can be obtained at www.ICGtesting.com
Printed in the USA
LVOW092036100412

277010LV00017B/141/P

9 781149 765203